by GEORGE PAPPADOPOULOS

Blackjack's Hidden Secrets II
George Pappadopoulos

ME-n-U Marketers
POB 127
Linwood, NJ 08221
Fax: 609-653-8186
Email: MEnUMark@aol.com

Find us on the World Wide Web at: http://www.blackjacknocounting.com

Graphic Designer: Rose De Dan, Cat Dancing Design
Cover Illustration: Alex Guillotte
Editor: Francine G. De Dan
Printer: Quick Stop Printing

Gambling Problem:
1-800-522-4700
in NJ 1-800-GAMBLER
in MO 1-888-BETSOFF

Pappadopoulos, George.
  Blackjack's hidden secrets II/ by George
  Pappadopoulos. -- 1st ed.
    p. cm.
    ISBN: 09673795-2-0

  1. Blackjack (Game)   I. Title.

GV1295.B55P37 2001   795.4'23
                    QBI01-200799
Library of Congress Control Number: 2001117721

First Printing 7/2001
Second Printing 9/2001
Third Printing 5/2002

Printed and bound in the United States of America.

Dedication

to Francine G. De Dan

No one has ever influenced my life more!
Her sole ability to calm the hurricane inside of me
is unique only to her.
She is truly the heart of this book!

Acknowledgments

Again I would like to thank all those who have contributed to my knowledge. Both of my books could not have been written without these gifted men. Among them are: Dr. Edward Thorpe, Ken Uston, Lawrence Revere, Julian Braun, Stanford Wong, Bobby Singer, Arnold Snyder, Jerry Patterson, Peter Griffin, Donald Schlesinger and John Patrick.

I would like to extend a special thanks to all the inquisitive blackjack players who have contacted me. Without your questions and thirst for more knowledge this second book would never have been written. Your emails, letters and phone calls brought many questions to the forefront and I hope I have been able to fulfill your curiosity.

Rose De Dan, Cat Dancing Design: Thank you for employing your command of the English language. It has been a fantastic experience watching my written words transform into a work with flow and grace.

Jay Massei, Quick Stop Printing: Thank you for your personal attention. You've made me feel like the largest fish in a small pond. Your fast service and ability to anticipate my most stringent demands have made you invaluable.

Mrs. D.: Thanks for coming through in a pinch...again!

Table of Contents

Preface

Fellow blackjack players, a few years ago I wrote my first book, *Blackjack's Hidden Secrets, Win Without Counting*. The system is still the same; it has not changed. You are probably asking, "If the rules haven't changed, why are you writing a second book? Answer: Since that first book, I have taken the system, maximized its usage, and expanded its potential in ways never imagined.

My goal for this book is to provide information not available in other blackjack books. Introduced here are my power play, sessions and the surrender option—all of which improve revenue and maximize the 78 percent win average.

Only here will you find information on blackjack tournaments (and a formula for winning), best places to play, and the different variations of blackjack (and why they are detrimental to the player). Also covered are topics such as intimidation (it's more prevalent than you might imagine), tipping and comps. Ever wish you could maximize your casino stay by receiving comps to get free rooms, free food and free shows? Here are some easy tips for this.

While I did not write this book for the professional blackjack player, I also cover how my system can be adjusted for such a career. Hopefully, you will be provided with sought after information—tools and weapons that will enable you to become a consistent winner like myself.

Sweetening the Pot
(casino freebies)

Comp is a short word for complementary, another way casinos entice players in to get their action. All casinos offer comps, but you have to be smart enough to receive them without being a high roller, or a loser. Before I tell you how, let me state emphatically that you are not there primarily to receive comps. Comps are the dessert after the meal. Winning, and winning consistently, is the meal and the reason you are there.

Comps are a way of maximizing your stay at the casino. Chasing them by betting over your head, or staying longer at a table just for a comp, is what the casinos want you to do. Don't play their game. Following my blackjack system correctly will make you enough money to reward yourself. Remember, comps are secondary, winning at blackjack primary. Once you win the casino's money you can become your own host and comp yourself. You are far better off a winner with a small comp than a loser with a large comp. Enough about the main course, now let me tell you about the variety of desserts that await you.

Free meals, free rooms and free shows: these are the freebies one can get just for asking, "ASKING" being the word. If you don't ask, you don't receive! I have been receiving these freebies (casinos call them "comps") for years now, and you can do the same by following a few simple steps.

Upon entering a casino, head directly for a house phone and ask for a casino host. Once you are in touch with a host, introduce yourself and ask to meet him or her. Tell them what you are wearing (so you are easily identifiable) and where you are located in the casino so he or she can meet you there.

Now, what should you wear? The first impression you make when meeting a host is of utmost importance (remember you only get one chance to make a first impression), so DO NOT wear sneakers and jeans. The mental picture you create now is the image that will surface the next time you contact your host. A suit (or sports jacket) and tie would be appropriate for the man, semi-formal to dressy-but-casual attire is suggested for the woman. Jewelry is a plus.

When meeting your host, smile, maintain eye contact and speak with authority. Remember: you are the guest and they are the host. Explain that this is your first time in their casino. Tell them you've heard how well they treat their guests and that their service is the best in the city. Tell them you've been going to another casino for years (name one—any one) and, although you've been treated very well at that casino, you can't seem to win (they like to hear that!). So, it was time to go elsewhere, and you selected their casino in hopes of changing your luck. Keep in mind that hosts will reward losing customers much more than winning ones, so cry a river of bad luck! It pays off.

By now you should have the host's attention and, due to the tremendous competition in the casino business, he or she will be eager to see what can be done to get your action and make you *their* customer. Here is where you need to be specific and know exactly what you want in the way of a comp, i.e., a meal, a room or a show. This is the *only* way you will get what you want.

Here are some examples: Tell your host you just got into town and would like to eat before beginning your casino play. Or tell him or her it's been a long day and you would like to relax with a few drinks and

♠ ♦ ♣ ♥

a show before you begin playing. Or, if you desire a room (Monday through Thursday being the best nights, unless it's a holiday), tell your host you just got into town and are interested in staying a couple days to try your luck. These scenarios should work for you at least once in every casino.

Now that you have your foot in the door, have met your host and have obtained your first comp, what comes next? Getting rated for more comps—and this means you need a player card. Every casino has a promotional booth which will issue you a card with your name and a player number, free of charge. The player number is how the casino keeps track of your play, which makes you eligible for comps. Comps are obtained by becoming a VIP, which, by casino definition, is someone who visits their casino once a month and plays a minimum of four hours over each 24-hour period. For example, if your stay is three days, you are expected to play four hours each day, not twelve hours in one day. This is the formula used to rate you for comps.

There are two categories of casino players: table players and slot players. Both differ when it comes to being rated for comps.

Unfortunately, the slot player is at a disadvantage. It is next to impossible to be rated higher than your actual play since the slot machine keeps track of your betting. If you choose to play slots (which I strongly advise against since it's the casinos' most lucrative game), you simply slide your card into the designated slot on the machine and your rating commences on your 1st spin. You will be rated by the amount of money you put in and the amount of time you play. When you have finished playing, simply remove your player card from the slot machine and the information it has gathered is used to calculate your comp monies.

♠ ♦ ♣ ♥

Table players have it much easier. They have the advantage of dealing with a person. Even though the pitboss, or the floor person, marks down your bets and records your playing time, they don't always see everything, which is to the table player's advantage.

So, how can you obtain comps in these situations without actually losing a lot of money? The tips presented here are applicable to any table game, but the examples used are based on blackjack since that is my game of choice. The comps I receive are a bonus to my winning, and I receive more than my fair share by following the techniques mentioned below.

With blackjack, the first thing you need to do is check the table trends (discussed in detail in my first book, *Blackjack's Hidden Secrets, Win Without Counting*). If the trends are favorable, give the floor person or pitboss your card before you begin playing. At that time they will enter your player information into the computer and begin rating your play. Your play is rated from the time they receive your card until the time you leave the table. If you switch tables, make sure the floor person or pitboss is aware of your move. The floor person keeps track of how much money you buy in with and how much you bet. Don't be too concerned with the table limit you are playing; all tables are ratable, it's just that higher action receives higher comps.

If possible, try to sit at a crowded table. Since you are rated on the amount of time you play, it makes sense that it takes longer to deal seven hands (usually the maximum seats) than five, for example. Additionally, shuffling is more frequent since more cards are being dealt. If possible stay away

♠ ♦ ♣ ♥

from tables with automatic card shufflers. These tables always have a dealable shoe since the machine does all the work. *Remember: time of play (expected four hours) is what's rated, not the number of hands you play.*

While at the table, nonchalantly take a chip or two (whenever possible) and hide it either in your pants pocket, coat, or wherever. Make certain the pitboss, floor person or dealer does not see this move. If you remove enough chips in this fashion throughout the night, the floor person will probably have you marked down as a loser by the end of your play (even though you've won) and will rate you a higher comp. *Remember: losers get higher comps than winners.*

Another move is to ask the dealer to place a lamer (that's a placeholder) in your spot while you go to the restroom. Collect your chips and leave for a short period of time. The lamer will hold your spot for approximately twenty minutes. When you return, don't put all your chips back on the table. This will give the impression that you've lost more money than you actually have. If you run out of chips buy in with more money, which will show a higher investment in your play.

Another method of stalling for time is to ask the dealer to deal you out for a couple hands while you collect your thoughts (this is also a good strategy for sitting out bad trends). Then resume your play. These moves buy you time and time gets you comps. A floor person won't close out your play for these brief pauses.

If you combine the tips I've given, you will be able to earn higher rewards than you deserve. I have enjoyed many freebies given by the casinos. Those

♠ ♦ ♣ ♥ 　　　5

freebies were in addition to remaining a winner 78 percent of the time I gamble. *Remember: comps are just sweet desserts and should not be the driving force of your main meal.* Your primary reason for being in a casino is to be a consistent winner— comps should just sweeten the pot.

♠ ♦ ♣ ♥

Dangerous Waters
(beware these blackjack systems)

CARD COUNTING

I strongly suggest leaving card counting to the professional. This is not a system to dabble in; it takes thousands of hours of practice to become proficient. To accomplish your goal you may have to give up your job, family, and friends, and travel around the country living out of a suitcase. Card counters are always in fear of being detected, which keeps them on the run. If discovered it could eliminate their occupation and source of revenue.

So, what is card counting? Card counting is simply the ability of the player to know how many 10-value cards are left in the shoe. This is done by giving the cards coming out of the shoe a number value. There are multitudes of sophisticated card counting systems. So as not to bore you with their technical aspects, I will address the simplest system possible in order to give you a clear picture of what card counting involves.

All card-counting systems use a plus-minus number system. For example, if you take a deck of cards and assign a +2 to 10-Jack-Queen-King and a -1 to 2-3-4-5-6-7-8-9 and keep a side count (separate count) of Aces, by the end of your 52-card deck you will have a count of 0 with a side count of 4 Aces. Whether you use one deck, four decks or eight decks, the system stays the same.

If the casino uses an 8-deck shoe the yellow cut card normally eliminates approximately two decks, so in your mind you are counting a six-deck shoe waiting for it to become rich with 10-value cards because they favor the player. When the shoe becomes rich, the counter ups his bet anywhere from ten to forty units, depending on the richness of the shoe, and takes two or more spots when possible. That's it. That's all counting is.

Sound easy? Well, it's not. Remember, it takes hundreds, if not thousands, of hours to become a proficient card counter, not to mention a huge bankroll so that when the shoe does become rich you have the ability to utilize the system. In order to make the system work your bankroll needs to be 600 times the table minimum. For example, to play at a $5 table you need a bankroll of $3000. Do you still want to be a card counter? Or better yet, can you afford to be one? If the answer is "yes" keep reading, it gets harder.

Casinos really try to pinpoint card counters since skilled players can hurt a casino. Their job is to detect and eliminate all the skilled players they can. To detect them the casinos use employees, cameras and even electronic devices. It begins with the dealer, who is trained to signal the floor person or pitboss if there is a suspected card counter at the table. The floor person or pitboss then begins observing the player, and they notify the eye in the sky. The next time you sit down to play blackjack look straight up, that large bubble overhead is the eye in the sky and it's got a camera watching over you.

At some point in time the casino calls in its card counting team. These are people employed by the casino who are expert card counters trained in detecting others. They observe your play for a few hands, and if they feel you're a counter they will call you to the side and tell you they don't want your action and ask you to leave the casino.

♠ ♦ ♣ ♥

And yes, they have the right to do this in every casino in the country *except* Atlantic City casinos. Atlantic City is the exception to the rule because in 1984 Ken Uston, who without a doubt is the greatest blackjack player who ever lived, took the Atlantic City casinos to the Supreme Court and won. He had it declared unconstitutional and discriminatory for a casino to ask a player to leave based on his skill.

To protect themselves the Atlantic City casinos took other defensive measures. When they suspect a card counter they now simply shuffle the cards after every hand which makes it impossible to count cards. Once the card counter realizes he has been detected he must now find another casino. The problem here is that the casinos share their information on card counters through photos from the eye in the sky and a complete description of the player. In Atlantic City, the counter has no place to go—every time he enters a casino and sits down to play blackjack he is recognized and the dealer is instructed to shuffle after every hand. Remember; this only applies in Atlantic City. Other casinos throughout the country just tap you on the shoulder and tell you to leave.

Also bear in mind that casinos share their information, not only with neighboring casinos, but also with every casino in the country! With these odds stacked against you, why learn something that you can't use? Eventually all card counters get caught, even when they work in teams of two to twenty players. There's no getting around it; card counting against today's technology is a losing proposition.

Are you ready for some good news? Unlike card counting, my non-card counting system is completely undetectable. I have been using it for many years in different casinos all over the country and have never been challenged or asked to leave. Casinos welcome me with comps—giving me free food, free rooms and free shows just to have a chance at my action. I ask you again, do you still want to be a card counter, or use my non-card counting system and win at blackjack?

THE MARTINGALE SYSTEM

Its theory leads you to believe that you will eventually win. Truth is you will wind up losing a lot more than you ever dreamed possible.

The idea behind this system is that if you lose your first bet you keep doubling the amount you bet until you win. The fact is you will run out of money before you realize that win.

Let me demonstrate why this is such a bad system. Let's say your first bet is $10. Using the Martingale System, if you lose, your next bet is $20, then $40-$80-$160-$320-$640-$1280-$2560, providing you lose each time. That's a possibility of nine losses in a row, which, by the way, is very possible. It has happened to me many times, although never at the same table, since my system only allows you to lose four times in a row at any one table before you leave that table and seek a friendlier one. It is possible that the next table may produce the same results, prompting you to move again, but, thank God, this doesn't happen often.

Let's compare the results of this happening with the Martingale System versus mine. Losing nine times in a row with the Martingale System results in a net loss of $5,110 and that's with an initial $10 bet. Losing nine times in a row with my system results

♠ ♦ ♣ ♥

in a $180 net loss, while this is disappointing, at least you're still in the game and have enough money left for that hot trend to happen.

Now say that by some chance you happen to win that bet at $2560, under the Martingale System you've just won a whole $10 and have risked $2560 to do it, since by this time, you have already lost a total of $2550. I don't know about you, but that's more money than I care to risk on that small a gain, keeping in mind your even having that much money to keep you going.

With the Martingale System it's more than a possibility that you'll be out of the game long before you can see your $10 gain. People lose houses this way. I know people who have used this system and have been so devastated that they will never play black-jack again.

My system is conservative, yet effective. It will not allow you to lose a large amount of money at any one session; however, it will make you a consistent winner with a 78 percent win average over a period of years. Bear in mind that I only look to win 50 percent of the bankroll I start with. In my first book, *Blackjack's Hidden Secrets, Win Without Counting* I state that poor discipline is the underlying reason why most people walk out of the casino losers. I would hate to see this happen to you, so don't be greedy, play with your head, not your heart.

Variety Is Not the Spice of Life
(beware these blackjack games)

Casinos are constantly coming up with different variations on the game of blackjack. All of these variations give the house a huge vig (or edge), some as high as 25 percent. The rules heavily favor the house but are camouflaged to appear as if they are giving players the edge. Don't be fooled by their very intelligent strategies. Think about it, why would the casino develop a game where you can beat them? Mega casinos are built by losers – not winners.

Covered below are five different games that should not be played by the non-counter. Two favor card counters, only because of the number of decks used, and the others are just bad news no matter how you look at them. Playing these games is suicide. You'd be better off sending the casino a check and not wasting your valuable time.

SINGLE DECK

Single deck blackjack hurts the non-card counter. The basic function of this game is to deflate the *card counter's* ability to make money. That said, let me explain how the game is played and why it removes any advantage for the non-counter. For this game the cards are dealt by hand rather than out of a shoe. The player receives two cards face down while the dealer receives one card face up and the other face down.

Rather than leaving the cards on the table the player picks up his two cards, and if he wants a hit, scratches the table with the cards. If he does not,

♠ ♦ ♣ ♥

he places them face down on the table, under his chips. If the player wants to split or double down he must turn his cards face up and put them on the table and instruct the dealer as to what he wants done. Nothing to panic about here.

This is where the casinos change the rules and, guess what, they're not in your favor! So pay attention. Do you remember the basic strategy chart, the chart that gives you the optimum moves for every hand so that you have an advantage? The casino changes these rules—they now only allow you to double down with a 10 or 11 and not with a 9. And remember those soft hands you could double down on, A-2, A-3, A-4, A-5, A-6, A-7? Gone. This is a huge disadvantage to the player. To add insult to injury, you are also not allowed to double down after a split. For example, if you split two 8's and you receive a 3 on your first 8 for a total of 11 and a 2 on your second 8 for a total of 10 you are not allowed to double down on either.

These rules drastically decrease your chances of leaving that table a winner. Remember, the reason the casino changes these rules is to diminish the skilled card counter's ability to multiply his money, because if left in place these rules could hurt the casinos. Obviously, you're not a card counter or you wouldn't be reading this book. So, why should you play a single deck game only to be punished by the casino and have them take away any portion of your opportunity to double down and double down after splits? These are two of the most powerful weapons you can have—by the casino taking any portion away it's like them giving you a brand new car with four bald tires and no spare. That new car won't take you very far, and neither will playing single deck blackjack.

DOUBLE DECK

Double deck blackjack is dealt and handled the same as single deck and the rules are essentially the same. The only difference, besides using two decks of cards, is that the casino now allows you to double down with an 8-9-10 or 11 where with single deck it was only 10 or 11. There is still no doubling down after splits or doubling with soft hands. Basically the only difference is they now allow you to double down with an 8 or 9. This is somewhat better, but if you remember your basic strategy you should never be doubling with an 8 in the first place. So the only thing you have gained is being able to double on a 9. Big deal! So now they've given you a new car with three bald tires and no spare. You may get a little farther down the road, but the end result is the same.

Take my advice, only play blackjack with cards that are dealt out of a shoe and it doesn't matter how many decks they use. I actually prefer to play with an eight-deck shoe so that when I hit a trend the ride is longer with fewer bumps along the way.

DOUBLE EXPOSURE

This so-called "great game" gives the house a 25 percent edge over you. The casino makes it look like they're doing you a favor because the dealer exposes both his cards. This sounds like a dream come true—knowing what the dealer's got—the catch: all ties go to the dealer. The only exception to this is your blackjack, which is an automatic win even if the dealer has blackjack. Unfortunately it only pays even money, unless you have an ace of spades and a jack of spades which then would pay you double. The chances of this are just about as

♠ ♦ ♣ ♥

good as you purchasing a garage sale painting and finding one of the original copies of the Constitution underneath.

Additionally, doubling down is only allowed with a 9,10, or 11— doubling with soft hands is not permitted. Allow me to illustrate how double exposure works: say the dealer has 19 and you have 19. Since all ties go to the dealer at this point you would lose. Therefore in any tie situation you would have to hit, even if basic strategy tells you not to. To beat the dealer in this scenario you must receive an ace or deuce, and the odds of you getting that are 6-to-1 against you.

The facts are that even if you play perfect basic strategy, for every 10 hands played you will win four, lose four and tie two. In double exposure, since all ties go to the dealer, this means that you will lose six out of 10 hands played which equates to 60 percent of the time. So by letting you see the dealers' two cards, the casino takes away any possibility of you beating them over the long haul and they know it. Knowing all this, ask yourself, do you still want to play double exposure?

MULTI BLACKJACK

A horrible game for the player, but a great game for the casino, giving them about a twenty percent vig. This game looks like regular blackjack except for the three circles located to the right side of the player. These circles are where your bets are placed, each bet being for the same amount of money. Here the dealer deals the player two cards and deals himself one. These two cards are now your hand, and you can play them as you would any hand of blackjack.

After you have played your cards, the dealer now gets three chances to beat your one hand. He begins with the first circle's bet, since he has only one card he draws another, say this card beats your hand, the dealer takes your first bet. He then discards the card he drew and draws another—he's now working on your second bet. Remember you still have the same hand. Again, his draw beats your cards; there goes another bet. The dealer is now down to your last bet. He repeats the process of drawing himself another card, and this time he breaks and you win. You actually get paid.

I know this sounds confusing so we'll run through an example. Let's say you have 18 and the dealer has 9. He draws a 10-value card giving him 19. At this point he takes your bet from the first circle. Moving to the next circle, the dealer still has a 9 and draws a 4 giving him 13, he hits again and draws a 7 which gives him 20. Since 20 beats 18 he takes your bet from the second circle. Now we're on our last bet. Remember, he still has a 9, so he hits and gets a 7 which gives him 16, draws another card and breaks. He then pays you the bet you have in the third circle.

Now there can be many combinations of whether you win or the dealer wins, but the odds are stacked against you. Playing this game makes it difficult to use basic strategy because some of the tried and true rules will put you at an even greater disadvantage by placing three bets on one bad hand. For example: if the dealer is showing a 7 or better you know with basic strategy that you have to hit until you reach a hard 17. The problem is if you get dealt a hard 14, 15 or 16 and you hit like you should, your odds of breaking are high, but with multi blackjack you now have three bets riding on this

♠ ♦ ♣ ♥

one hand so if you do break you lose all three. Most blackjack players will take a look at this and NOT have the guts to follow basic strategy because of the three bets. The difficulty is that if you don't hit, your odds of losing are even greater than your odds of breaking. A great case of damned if you do, and damned if you don't.

In essence with multi blackjack the player risks three bets on a single hand while the dealer gets three different hands. Although a better game than double exposure, the end result is the same, you still go home a loser, it just takes longer.

If your reason for playing multi blackjack is to increase your return, do yourself a favor and play a basic game of blackjack and just increase your wager. This way one bad hand won't cost you three bets. Also keep in mind that if you do play this game you need three times the bankroll (defined in my first book), because this game is like playing three seats without the advantage of three different hands.

SPANISH 21

Spanish 21 is a trendy game; it's only been around for about five years. Its birthplace is Las Vegas but it has spread like the plague throughout the majority of casinos in the country. Its popularity is due to the fact that the average blackjack player cannot see the forest for the trees, and it seems like a great way to beat the casino.

In my opinion, this is the most deceptive blackjack game in the casino. On the surface the rules look like the next best thing to sliced bread, but as you dig deeper you'll find the bread is not sliced all the way through. They have taken away your knife to cut

♠ ♦ ♣ ♥

the bread (the 10's) and try to hide it by offering you all these other great rules. If you could play basic blackjack with these rules you'd slaughter them. Without these 10's, Spanish 21 gives the house a 25 percent vig. You will lose your money faster at this blackjack game than in any other. Listen to some of the rules, tell me if they don't tempt you, but keep in mind that you are playing without any 10's.

Spanish 21 is dealt just like regular blackjack. That is where the similarity ends. Spanish 21 is the only game left with late surrender (which I cover in an upcoming chapter). The surrender option is available on any of the player's first two cards, just like surrender in any other game. The difference is that if the dealer has blackjack, and you have surrendered your hand, you lose only half your bet.

Another interesting move in Spanish 21 is that they allow you to double down after drawing your third card. Where have you ever heard of that? For example: if you have a 4 and a 3 and you draw a 4 so you now have a total of 11 this game lets you double down. Seems to get better with every sentence, doesn't it?

To further entice you, and this game is loaded with enticements, they have an option called rescue, which is similar to surrender but is used only after doubling down. For example: you've been dealt a 4 and a 3, you hit this and get another 4 so you now have 11, the perfect opportunity to double down. Of course you do and receive an Ace. What are you going to do with a 12? Use "rescue." Now you only lose half your bet. Sounds like you can't lose, right? Wrong, but that's what they want you to think. Remember; there are no 10's in this game.

♠ ♦ ♣ ♥

Another bonus Spanish 21 has is that if you are dealt three 7's you get paid 5-to-1 on your bet and if you get three 7's of the same suit, like 3 spades or 3 hearts, you get paid $2500 on the spot. You're probably asking can the game of blackjack get any better than this? Remember the word I used in the beginning of this section, "deception?" The casinos are great at it.

The odds of you getting those three 7's in a row are 1300-to-1 against you, ask any poker player, they will verify this, and the odds of being dealt three 7's of the same suit are 662,000-to-1. Now I didn't pull those figures out of the air, they are mathematic fact proven by putting one billion hands of blackjack into a computer and calculating the percentages. The casinos know these odds, but think you don't, so they try to hook you in with fantastic promises in order to lure *your* money into *their* pockets.

So far most of the rules I have mentioned have been positive for the player, you are probably saying to yourself what makes Spanish 21 a terrible game to play, and how can the casino have a 25 percent edge when all the rules favor the player? The answer: *the casinos have removed all the 10's in the shoe and remember Spanish 21 is played with an 8-deck shoe.* There are still jacks, queens and kings but no 10's. That, and that alone, makes it possible for the casino to obtain their 25 percent vig from this game.

Let me explain how detrimental no 10's can be. With no 10's in the shoe, it gives you, the player, 32 less chances of getting blackjack. It also gives you 32 fewer chances to double down with a 9, 10 or 11 and receive a 10-value card. Last but not least, and certainly the most important, it reduces the dealers'

♠ ♦ ♣ ♥

chances of breaking. Remember the dealer must hit until he reaches a hard 17, so without those 10's to make him break, his odds of getting low value cards in order to beat you are fantastic. Now do you understand why the casino loves you to play Spanish 21?

Please try to understand that if Single and Double Deck Blackjack, Spanish 21, Multi Blackjack and Double Exposure did not so heavily favor the casino, they simply would not exist. Casinos make hundreds of millions of dollars by legal deception. If you think these games are too good to be true, you're right. If you want to beat the casino at blackjack, like I do, with a 78 percent win average, play only basic blackjack, using my system, and leave the modified versions for someone else.

♠ ♦ ♣ ♥

Surrender Is Not Submission

Always, always, always play at a casino that offers surrender. Surrender enables the player to pull back half his bet when the dealer has a strong hand and the player a weak one. This option can only be implemented on your first two cards.

In the 1980's, every casino in Atlantic City offered surrender. As years passed all but the Claridge did away with it. Surrender, it turns out, became too powerful a move in favor of the player. The Claridge, being a small casino, kept it in order to compete with the big guys. By being the only casino in town to have surrender, the smart blackjack player is drawn there. Their thinking: give up a little to get a lot.

You may ask yourself, how strong is this option? Surrender gives the player an additional quarter of one percent of an edge over the casino. It may not sound like a lot but in the long haul it could mean the difference between walking out a winner versus a loser. The casinos recognize how powerful this is, so instead of taking the risk most have chosen to do away with this option.

There are two types of surrender—early surrender and late surrender. The difference is simple. In early surrender if the dealer has blackjack you lose your entire bet; in late surrender you only lose half. Late surrender is really not a concern; I have played in numerous casinos and have yet to see it offered. Of the casinos that still have surrender, the late option was done away with years ago because it greatly increased the players' odds. The only exception to this is in Spanish 21, which was covered earlier.

♠ ♦ ♣ ♥   21

Imagine being in a bad trend (which happens to all of us at one time or another) having a hard 15 or 16 against the dealer's picture or Ace and losing only half your bet. When you are able to use surrender, this could turn what might have been a losing night into a winning one. I can't tell you how many times I've watched someone lose by not using this option while I've won.

One night stands out in particular. I was at the Claridge, playing at a $50 table, sitting at first base. At third base was this self-proclaimed blackjack expert who gave me a hard time whenever I used the surrender option. When the situation was appropriate I would surrender my hand and get back half my bet rather than risk losing my entire bet on a bad percentage hand. For example: I would surrender a hard 16 against a dealer's picture card.

The person at third base would tell me I didn't know what I was doing and that surrender favored the house. That's why they offered it. I tried to explain what a strong move it was for the player and pointed out that if surrender favored the house then every casino in Atlantic City would have it. He told me I was crazy and that I should be playing at a $5 table with the other rookies. He further went on to say that only skilled players like himself should be allowed to play at the high limit tables.

Upon hearing this I gave up any hope of converting this blackjack guru to reality and continued to play the way I always do. I don't allow what a person says or how they play their hand to distract me; I focus on my game and let everyone else play their own. Within one hour I reached my win goal of $1000, colored in my chips and got up to leave. At this time I overheard the blackjack guru who had been heckling me tell his buddy that he'd lost $2500 and it

♠ ♦ ♣ ♥

was time to go. At that point we made eye contact and I said to him, "It's amazing how a great player like you lost and a terrible player like me won." He looked at me, hesitated and then said, "You're not a fool, I am. I watched you play and you're good. Be assured, the next time I come here I'll use surrender." He then offered his hand and I shook it. I went to the cashier cage, cashed in my chips and called it a night, a very good night.

In the chart below I have outlined the rules for using surrender and hope that by now you are getting a feel for how powerful a weapon this option this can be. This chart comes from the same mathematical statistics that basic strategy is derived from. I suggest you commit it to memory, but just in case you have a memory lapse, there is a tear-out chart located in the back of the book. You may bring this chart to the blackjack table and refer to it whenever in doubt. Remember surrender is not submission, it is POWER.

Surrender if:

DEALER HAND	YOUR HAND
Ace	5, 6, 7, 12 thru 17 or two 8's
Ten value card	14, 15, 16 or two 8's
9	(10, 6) or (9, 7) - split two 8's

Never surrender soft hands.

♠ ♦ ♣ ♥

Blackjack Tournaments

I think they're fantastic. I seek them out whenever possible. They are a great way to maximize a trip to the casino. I have been playing in blackjack tournaments all over the country for years and also on cruise ships.

I must warn you that you have to be very careful when playing tournaments on cruise ships. Make certain you check the rules against the ones I mention here and if they don't match, don't play. Cruise ships are unregulated so they can make up their own rules and do not have to follow standard tournament procedures.

By using my tournament system I can almost assure you a seat in the final round. If you've ever played tournaments you know that everyone in that round makes money. Best of all, you won't believe how easy it is. Remember simplicity is the key to success and it can't get any simpler than what I'm going to tell you.

Tournament blackjack is a head game; you're not playing against the casino you're playing against the other players at your table. The object, believe it or not, is to be passive not aggressive. When I play other players think I'm a novice, like someone who has never played blackjack before, and guess what? That's what I want them to think. Before they realize what I'm doing the tournament is over and I'm in the money. This is a case where the less people think you know the more powerful you will become. As I said before, this is a head game. If you like playing poker, you'll love playing tournament blackjack.

♠ ♦ ♣ ♥

I've found that most casinos throughout the country have blackjack tournaments at least once a week—some have entry fees and others are by invitation only. If you find that the casino you happen to be at doesn't offer any tournaments, either ask around or pick up the phone and start calling other casinos near you. In the larger casino resort areas you should be pleasantly surprised to find at least one or more within walking distance. On board ship they should have at least one blackjack tournament on every cruise.

The casinos know that blackjack is their most popular game, they also know that the players want tournaments. What blackjack player wouldn't want the opportunity to possibly win a few thousand dollars for an investment of as little as $25 and their time? Without blackjack tournaments a player could become disgruntled and seek out another casino that has them—that's the last thing the casinos want. They spend millions of dollars on advertising to get players into their casino so they can benefit from the player's action. What purpose would be served not giving players what they want?

Essentially blackjack tournaments don't cost the casino anything; the prize money is derived from the players' entry fee, normally about $25. Now you might be thinking, it does cost the casino something. They have to provide the space to play and the dealer to deal the cards. Well, the space is already there and the dealers are minimum wage. Don't ever underestimate the casinos' ulterior motive, they're anything but Good Samaritans. Giving something for nothing is not in their vocabulary. The average blackjack tournament has 216 players. Ask yourself this question, what would 216 blackjack players do after a tournament is over and they are surrounded with blackjack tables? If you said play blackjack, you're right. Casinos aren't stupid; they've figured this out, too.

At this time I would like to discuss the rules of a blackjack tournament. They are dry, so try to bear with me, after that I'll show you how to optimize your chances. It's so easy you'll be shocked. These rules are prevalent in most blackjack tournaments. They may vary slightly from casino to casino but not enough to make a difference.

In most cases you sign up one hour before the tournament begins, or if you happen to be there a day or so early, you can make arrangements with a pit-boss and pay ahead of time to ensure your spot. Entry fees are usually $25. This entitles you to tournament chips and an opportunity to win one of six prizes. The prize break down is as follows.

1st **place:**   40% of all monies in the cash prize pool

2nd **place:**   20% of all monies in the cash prize pool

3rd **place:**   15% of all monies in the cash prize pool

4th **place:**   12% of all monies in the cash prize pool

5th **place:**   8% of all monies in the cash prize pool

6th **place:**   5% of all monies in the cash prize pool

One hundred percent of the prize pool money is divided amongst the top six players, so if you're in the final round you come out with cash in hand.

ROUND 1 is twenty hands. There are usually twelve tables that start in this round. The winner is determined by who has the most money at the end of the twenty hands. This person advances to Round 2. Participants that do not advance to Round 2 may opt to play in the Re-Buy Round (second chance

♠ ◆ ♣ ♥

round) for an additional $15 dollars. The Re-Buy Round starts as soon as the first round is complete. You must have participated in Round 1 to play in the Re-Buy Round. The Re-Buy Round is fifteen hands and the highest winner from each table will also advance to Round 2. There is only one Re-Buy Round.

ROUND 2 is fifteen hands and the winner from each table advances to the Semi-Final Round.

SEMI-FINAL ROUND is fifteen hands and the winner from each table advances to the Final Round.

FINAL ROUND is also fifteen hands. Here six participants play for the aforementioned prizes.

- At the start of the First and Second Round all participants receive $500 in tournament chips (amount may be higher).

- Participants in the Semi-Final and Final Round receive $1000 in tournament chips (amount may be higher).

- All participants must play every hand.

- First Round, Re-Buy and Second Round minimum bet is normally $5 and the maximum bet $500.

- Semi-Final and Final Round minimum bets are normally $5 and the maximum bet $1000.

At this time I want you to remember the word minimum bet. It's so important that I want you to repeat the word *minimum bet* ten times out loud. I'll talk more about this later.

The tournament chips you are given must be kept in view at all times and in an orderly fashion. They must be visible to the dealer as well as all of the participants at the table. If you keep them in your hand or put them in your pocket you'll be disqualified. Tournament chips cannot be given to another player and must be returned to the dealer at the end of each round. These chips have no cash value so there is really no reason to hold on to them.

All games are dealt with a single hand-held deck (not from a shoe). All cards are dealt face up with the exception of the dealer's second card. Players may double down on any two cards including Ace combinations. Players may split four times (including Aces). Players may take insurance. Blackjack pays double in a tournament, not 1½ times your bet.

Player Puck – A "First Player" puck is used to indicate where the first hand will be dealt. The decision of who will be the first player at the beginning of each round will be determined by a draw of cards—high card is first base (Aces high). The puck will move around the table one position, after each hand (clockwise from the dealer's left). The dealer will always receive the last card. The deck will be shuffled after each hand. Only the player who is first base (with the puck) will cut the cards. If they are unwilling to cut the dealer will make the cut.

For the last five hands the players must place their bets in order, starting with whoever is first base. First player puck bets cannot be changed once the bet is in the circle and the player's hand is no longer touching the bet.

First Round: The dealer will notify the players at the halfway point when there are ten hands left to play. At this point the dealer will have all players count down their bankrolls, and the dealer will announce the amounts to the table.

All rounds: the dealer will notify the players when there are five hands left to play and again have the play-

♠ ♦ ♣ ♥

ers count down their bankrolls, and the dealer will announce the amount to the table. Tournament chips will be counted at the end of each round to determine who will advance to the next round. Ties will be broken by a draw of cards—high card wins (Aces high). All advancing players will be assigned a table and seat number for the next round. All advancing players will receive chips when seated at the next round.

Late arrivals for the first round: seat assignments will be sold if there is a waiting list, otherwise the late arrivals will start with chips of an equal amount to the player with the least chips minus $10 on that particular table. In all other rounds, late arrivals start with chips of an equal amount to the player with the least chips on that particular table, minus $10. During tournament play discussions or coaching between players and or spectators is prohibited in order to give all players an equal chance. In the event a dispute arises, the tournament committee will render a decision, and each entrant must accept all decisions of the committee as final and binding. The management will disqualify any participant for misconduct or infractions of published rules.

That's it, those are the general rules throughout a blackjack tournament. They many vary slightly, but insignificantly, from tournament to tournament, not enough to make a difference.

Now that we've gone through the laundry list of rules and regulations, it's time to find out how easy it is to get to the final round and make you one of the winners. Here is my formula for achieving that goal. Let's start with Round 1. If you've ever watched a tournament you've probably noticed that 99 percent of the players play very aggressively.

With the first hand they begin betting big money. This makes no sense to me since they're playing against each other, not against the casino. You'll also see that they have no money management, and very little discipline.

When you play my tournament system I want you to bet the minimum bet until you get to the last five hands at which time the dealer will announce "five hands left" and will instruct each player to count their chips and announce their totals at that time.

Let me draw you a picture. At the beginning of the tournament the officials will start you with either a $500 or $1000 bank. For our example say it's $1000. Your minimum bet is $5 and your maximum bet is $1000. I repeat again, *only bet the minimum* each hand, which will be $5, until you reach the last five hands. I know I sound redundant and you think I may be crazy, but *this is key to being a winner in the tournament*. In the first round, the tournament starts with six players at your table. By the time the dealer announces "five hands left" there will probably be only three players at your table, yourself and two others. Because of their aggressive betting the other three will have lost all their chips and be out of the tournament.

Here is an example, if you begin with a $1000 bank, play fifteen out of twenty hands at $5 per hand and lose all of them you still have $925 left in chips. The probability is that you will have more money left than the other two remaining players will. If not, adjustments need to be made in your betting at that time. The betting strategy that I recommend has given you the ability and opportunity to do so because you have only bet $5 per hand for the first fifteen hands. Didn't I tell you it was a head game? You *can* beat a more seasoned player than yourself

♠ ♦ ♣ ♥

by simply following my instructions. With only five hands left you still bet only the minimum bet, which is $5, for your next two hands. I'm sure by now you're very nervous and your heart is beating like you just ran a marathon. That's perfectly normal, just keep your cool and listen to me. Up to this point you should be following strict basic strategy. When you have reached the last three hands, regardless of what round it is, basic strategy does a little transformation. Splitting and doubling down are now *not* options when using my technique.

You now have three hands left to play and remember the PUCK is still being passed around. This is very important since it determines who bets first so you can better judge how much money you will need either to stay ahead, if that's where you are, or catch up. At this point you look and count the remaining players' chips. If they have less money than you and they bet first, when it comes your time to bet you must calculate how much money you need to put up in order beat them by $5— you must assume they will win. For example: the player closest to you in money has $800 and you have $900, they decide to bet $400 so if they win they'll have $1200, this means you would need to bet $305, giving you $1205, just enough to beat them if you both win. On the flip side, if you're ahead of the other players and you have to bet first just bet the minimum, $5, let them chase you. You still have two hands left if you need to adjust your strategy.

In the situation where they have more money than you do, if you are betting first you should put up half your bankroll. In doing this you have jumped out of character and have thrown the other players off guard; they won't know what to think. This amount also allows you money for the last two hands. In the situation where you are betting last, you must calculate how much you need to put up to beat the other players. This is calculated by looking to see which player would be in the lead if they won their bet. You need to put up enough to tie that bet plus $5. For example: they have $900 and you have $700. They put up a bet of $400, which means that if they win they have $1300. This means that you need to put up $605, enough to tie them and come ahead by $5. In the event you do not have enough to cover that bet you must put up your entire bankroll.

Now with only two hands left to play you will need to follow the same procedure as stated above, making whatever adjustments necessary to stay ahead by $5, even if it means going to the maximum bet of $1000.

Now you're up to the last hand for this round. Only bet enough chips to win; again based on the procedures above—don't bet everything you have, because in most cases you don't have to. It's very possible you can lose the last hand and the other player can win the last hand, but you will win this round because you have the most money at the end of the game. At this point you should be able to pat yourself on the back and put a smile on your face because you've just made it closer to the final round. The rounds to follow are played the exact same way, and if you've taken my advice you should be gleefully holding money in your hand.

When I told you how easy it is to win a tournament at the beginning of this chapter you probably had your doubts. Remember, in blackjack tournaments it's not the best player that wins, it's the smartest. There's a lot of easy money to be made playing blackjack tournaments. All you have to do is be

♠ ♦ ♣ ♥

calm and cool, and follow my guidelines. One more thing, if you meet another player at your table doing exactly what I just told you to do, ask them if they've read my book—this way you'll know what you're up against.

Conquering Intimidation

Intimidation runs rampant in every casino, more so at blackjack tables than in any other game. There are three types of intimidation when it comes to gambling: casino intimidation, dealer intimidation, and player intimidation. I know many people who won't play blackjack anymore for fear of being intimidated. They have turned to slots (the worst game in the casino) because they can sit down in peace without fear of the slot machine talking back to them.

One of the best ways to avoid intimidation is to have a solid foundation in blackjack. My first book, *Blackjack's Hidden Secrets, Win Without Counting* has given many people that foundation. I have received e-mails from people who had switched to slots because of feeling intimidated at the black-jack table and are now back to the tables because of their newly-found confidence. One lady wrote, "Instead of being talked down to by the dealer and other players I am now looked up to, and asked what move would I make if I were them."

Casino intimidation begins as you approach the casino. The first thing you see is this high structure with wall-to-wall neon lights, some blinking some not. As you walk through the doors you hear whistles, bells and the ding-ding-ding of the slot machines. You are surrounded by chandeliers, marbled walls and an escalator with real flowers and plants seem to grow out of its' sides. Passing through the slot area, on your way to the table games, you hear people yelling and screaming. There are employees dressed in different uniforms, from formal tuxedos with starched white shirts to polo shirts with the casino's logo on them, and the

♠ ♦ ♣ ♥

cocktail waitresses, whose uniforms are half the length of a mini skirt and leave little on the top to the imagination. For someone who has never been to a casino, this can be an overwhelming and humbling experience. This type of intimidation can be overcome, first by making yourself aware that these things are all done to distract you and keep you off balance, and secondly by becoming more familiar with the surroundings.

The remaining two types of intimidation are much harder to deal with since they involve human interaction.

Let us move on to dealer intimidation, which I've seen quite often. Imagine a hot-shot dealer, who just finished a three-month schooling on dealing blackjack, trying to rush your decision on a move at the blackjack table. They don't look at you; they stare at you, and sometimes roll their eyes because they feel you're taking too long to make up your mind.

Then you have the speed dealer who thinks he's in the casino Olympics. He's either showing off or believes that by being the fastest dealer in the casino he'll be promoted more quickly. In my experience dealers are promoted based on friendliness and accuracy, not speed.

Then there is the dealer who passes you by, assuming you're going to stay with your hand when you haven't given a hand signal of any kind. One time, when it happened to me, I asked the dealer, "Are you psychic? How did you know what I was going to do?" His answer was, "I just knew by the way you play." This should *never* happen; it's YOUR money. Don't let the dealer play YOUR hand.

Another experience etched in my memory is the time I had a 19 and the dealer had 18. He took my money, discarded the cards and began to deal another hand. I told the dealer I won that hand, the dealer said I was wrong. I then stood up, called the floor person over, and asked him to back up the cards from the discard holder. The floor person did as I asked, found me to be correct, apologized, gave me back my money plus my win for the bet. The dealer's only response was: "How did that happen?" He never apologized, and, acting like nothing had happened, began dealing another hand. The lady next to me said, "Bravo," and patted me on the back. She then whispered in my ear, "I would never have said anything." I asked her why; her reply, "I wouldn't want to get the dealer mad at me."

This is the most blatant case of dealer intimidation I've ever come across. It gives real meaning to the word intimidation, when the fear of retaliation from a dealer becomes greater than the desire to fight for the money you've just won. I know that this can be difficult at times, but let me remind you IT'S YOUR MONEY! And you're the only one who is going to lose by letting these things happen.

If any of these situations should happen at your table you have two choices, first is to tell the floor person or pitboss what the problem is so he can rectify it with the dealer. Trust me, he will speak to the dealer and resolve the problem. Second, if you are afraid of a confrontation with the dealer, floor person, or pitboss, you have no other choice but to leave the table and find a dealer friendlier to your needs. Keep in mind that you must be comfortable and relaxed in order to play your best, and unless you're a masochist, staying at that table is not an option.

Last, but not least, is player intimidation. This is the most common form of intimidation you will encounter in the casino while playing blackjack.

♠ ♦ ♣ ♥

Most blackjack players think they're good, some think they're great. The fact is that most blackjack players don't even know basic strategy. Few have a money management formula, very few have a good money management formula, and almost none have good discipline.

Keep this in mind when another player questions your play or tries to belittle you; ask him if he's so good at blackjack, what's his win average? Most times this won't shut him up; however, it should quiet him down. We all know them, in all walks of life these people are referred to as know-it-alls, jacks-of-all-trades-and-masters-of-none. They're usually obnoxious, boisterous, and irritating. If a player continues to talk down to you, or tell you how to play, answer back by saying "Look buddy (or miss), this is the way I play. I will continue to play this way as long as I'm here. If you don't like it find another table because I'm not changing my play." I can almost guarantee that within the next couple of hands this irritant will get up, go to another table, and most likely find someone else to taunt. If this doesn't happen, and you're becoming irritated yourself, the best move is to move. Remember you are supposed to be comfortable.

Intimidation is a horrible feeling, and mastering the effect it has on you can change your entire experience at the casino. As I mentioned at the beginning of this chapter, intimidation has chased players away from the blackjack table and on to slots—don't let this happen to you.

Tipping–When, Why, and How Much

In the hospitality industry the definition of the word "tips" is "to insure prompt service." In the casinos there are only two people I tip, the dealer and the cocktail waitress. I do this discriminately. Not all dealers are equal, and not all cocktail waitresses are friendly, so I tip accordingly.

Both dealers and cocktail waitresses rely heavily on tips. Their salary is based on the minimum wage, and in some casinos they get paid below minimum wage because they are a tipped position. The cocktail waitresses may keep whatever they make, however dealers must pool their tips whether they deal blackjack, craps, roulette, baccarat, or any other game. This is prevalent throughout every casino in the country. The casino comes up with the "TOKE" rate; this is the total amount of the pooled money, divided by the total amount of hours worked by all dealers.

The toke rate varies from week to week depending on the amount of tips. Each dealer then gets paid the toke rate times the amount of hours they worked that week. For example: a dealer who has worked 30 hours gets less than a dealer who has worked 40 hours, however the hourly toke rate is still the same. Now put this in your memory bank, *the amount of your gratuity has no bearing on your play*. The dealer is still going to shuffle the cards the same way, and deal them precisely according to the rules of the game. Therefore, if you believe that by tipping him more it will enhance your chances of winning, banish that thought. I know that sometimes it seems that if you are good to the dealer he'll be good to you. This is a nice thought, but not very logical. The

♠ ♦ ♣ ♥

reason you tip is for a job well done, not because you think it will change the cards.

The amount you tip varies, depending on player generosity. When I win, my standard gratuity is anywhere between two to five percent of my winnings, and that's not until the end of my session, after I color my chips and am ready to leave. I do this for a reason. I don't believe in tipping while I am playing as so many other players do. Bear in mind, I brought an exact bankroll to the casino to play blackjack at the table limit my bankroll allows. If I were to tip the dealer every five or six hands played, I would greatly jeopardize my chances of winning since I would have depleted my bankroll.

I can't tell you how many times I've been near the bottom of my bankroll before I hit the hot trend that first brought me back to even, and then achieved my win goal. If I hadn't had this money behind me it would have greatly diminished my chances of leaving the casino a winner. I am a strong advocate of the dealer getting his, but I want mine first. It's my money at risk, and I want to make certain my investment pays off. For example: if you are playing at a table that has an 8-deck shoe with six other players, the dealer averages 60 hands dealt in one hour. If you were to tip one dollar after every five hands, you would be giving away $12 an hour. In a three-hour period your bankroll would have decreased by $36. This deficit could make the difference between your walking out a winner or leaving a loser. You could have the hottest trend in the world, but what good is it if you don't have the money to play it?

I've explained to you how I tip when I win, losing is a different story all together. I just don't do it; there is no reason to, and the dealers understand this. In their hearts they know that when you win, they win. Two to five percent of your winnings is a good tip, and the dealer will remember you and hope you come back again.

I'll bet you thought I forgot the cocktail waitress, not so. I always bring an extra two or three dollars with me that is not counted in my bankroll, so that when I want a cup of coffee or soft drink I can tip the cocktail waitress upon the arrival of my drink. I always tip one dollar per drink whether I'm winning or losing. It shows proper etiquette. You don't want to be regarded as a mooch just because the drinks are free. And remember, I said coffee or a soft drink. As I stress in my first book, DO NOT drink alcohol before your play, or during your play. That means no beer, wine or mixed drinks. There's plenty of time for that after you win and leave the table. Don't give the casino any more of an edge than they already have.

♠ ♦ ♣ ♥

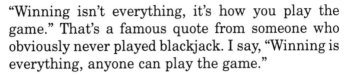

Preferred Places to Play
(the best places to win your money)

"Winning isn't everything, it's how you play the game." That's a famous quote from someone who obviously never played blackjack. I say, "Winning is everything, anyone can play the game."

In the United States alone, there are hundreds of casinos, and more being built every day. There are hundreds of cruise ships in the water, each (except for Disney) having a casino on board. You don't even have to leave your home, just log on to the Internet, and play blackjack to your hearts content while dressed in your robe and slippers.

Having gambled in casinos all over the country, and cruised the waters of many islands, I feel qualified to give you my opinion as to which casinos and cruise liners offer the best rules for the player. I have played in many but now only frequent a few. The following properties mentioned are locations where the blackjack rules favor the player. At this point I would like to make it clear that I do not receive any royalties or special consideration for highlighting these casinos. I wrote this book for you, the player, so you might share my experience of being a consistent winner.

NEVADA

Las Vegas	Lake Tahoe	Reno
a. Palace Station	a. Caesar's Casino*	a. Harrah's Casino
b. Gold Coast Casino	b. Horizon Casino	b. Harvey's Casino

NEW JERSEY
Atlantic City
Claridge Casino*

Bally's Park Place (Wild West) Casino

Tropicana Casino

CONNECTICUT
Mohegan Sun Casino*

CRUISE LINES
Royal Caribbean

Carnival

* these casinos offer surrender

You are probably asking yourself "How about the Belausio in Vegas, or the Taj Mahal in Atlantic City?" and many others I didn't mention. Just because they are magnificent mega casinos with singing water displays or gigantic statues that move and talk, it doesn't mean they're going to have the best blackjack rules for you—actually it can be just the opposite. You might find that the rooms are more beautiful, and that they have more amenities than the one you're staying in, but in the long run somebody has to pay for these perks (guess who).

If you want something to remember them by, take a lot of pictures, and then move on to the casinos I have recommended and play blackjack. When you get home you'll have beautiful pictures and a wallet full of money. A picture is worth a thousand words, however money is what makes the world go 'round. One more thing about those lavish rooms the mega casinos have, ask yourself, when you go on vacation, how many waking hours do you spend in your

♠ ♦ ♣ ♥

room? Probably very little. You can have the best of both worlds; make the money at the casinos I recommend, and reward yourself with gourmet dining and headliner shows with profits of your play.

Cruising, what a great way to get away from it all. Of the many cruises I have taken I can't say I've been on a bad one yet. I enjoy visiting different ports of call in the day, and playing blackjack at night. Unlike land-based casinos, the ones on board ship are normally only allowed to operate while at sea.

It has been my experience that the rules for blackjack are the same on all cruise lines. These rules are good for the player but not great. I will say though that if any discrepancies come up, they are usually willing to give the player the benefit of the doubt unlike land-based casinos. Cruise casinos are on board ships mainly for your enjoyment, so they are more lenient since it's not their primary means of revenue. They really are concerned with your having a good time.

These ships do offer blackjack tournaments, but before deciding to play reread the chapter on tournament blackjack to make sure they have regulation rules. Cruising can be both profitable and fun. It's like having your cake and eating it too.

Last, but not least, the Internet. I have been told by several people my system works great online. Many practice my strategies on the web before going into a live casino. There are others who prefer to play at home and have e-mailed me boasting how well they've done. Personally I enjoy the action of a live game and with many casinos close by, why do otherwise? The information highway is a great tool, but I use it only to gather information. So there you have it, this is who I am, where I go, and what I do.

♠ ♦ ♣ ♥

Sessions versus My Power Play
(extended play for the passive or aggressive player)

♥

I teach a lot of seminars, am interviewed regularly on radio and answer a lot of e-mail since my first book, *Blackjack's Hidden Secrets, Win Without Counting*. One of the questions I get asked most frequently deals with what a player is supposed to do after he or she has reached their win goal but is not in a position to go home.

The scenario goes something like this: "I'm on vacation, I reached my win goal in thirty minutes and you say I'm supposed to go home. Well, I can't, home is 2000 miles away, so what am I supposed to do now?" This is an excellent question, one I have given much thought, and have come up with two choices. Through research I have developed sessions for the passive player, and the power play for the aggressive player.

SESSIONS

I recommend sessions for 90 percent of the black-jack players who use my system. I suggest sessions because there's less risk involved. I have developed a way that you can maximize your stay, get all the blackjack action you want, and still have plenty of time to spend on fun things while you're away from home. Now I know that many of you consider blackjack fun, but if you want to become a consistent winner you must take it seriously.

Here's how it works. Let's say you are on vacation or a business trip for any period of time and there is a casino near where you are staying, which in today's day and age is more probable than not.

♠ ♦ ♣ ♥

You're looking to play blackjack but you don't know how much money to bring. To calculate your bankroll for either an overnight stay or a one-month excursion I will use a $5 table as an example. If you've read my first book you already know that the proper bankroll is 40 times the table minimum, therefore you need $200 to play one session. The definition of a session is that you have either reached your win goal (50 percent of your bankroll) or your loss limit (100 percent of your bankroll). If you wish to play two sessions a day at the $5 table you need a bankroll of $400; $200 per session. If you wish to play three sessions per day you need $600 as a total bankroll per day. If your trip is for four days, and you're planning on playing two sessions per day, you would need a total bankroll of $1600. If you are looking to play a higher table limit the formula is: (40 times the table minimum) x (the number of sessions you want to play in a day) x (the amount of days of your stay.)

Allow me to point out, that even for the most avid blackjack player, I do not recommend more than three sessions a day. I know myself that my brain begins to hurt if I play that much blackjack.

You must keep in mind that session play can vary in length tremendously. I strongly suggest no more than two sessions per day, which should give you plenty of action and time for other things. Playing blackjack requires brainpower, so don't wear yourself out prematurely. The casinos are open 24/7 and will be around for a lot longer than either you or I.

It has been my experience that an average session lasts about two hours, and that's two hours of actual play. It doesn't count the time you spend checking table trends or walking around the casino. Your session is over when you have either hit your win goal or reached your loss limit—in either case you must leave the casino. *At no time should you stay at a hot table if you're winning or use other session money if you lose.* You must leave the casino. You need this time to recharge your energy. This may sound wrong to you, but if you want to become a consistent winner you must follow my rules.

The waiting time between sessions is a minimum of two hours; I recommend three, before you start again. You have to clear your mind and you can do this any number of ways. Go to a restaurant, take a swim, see a show or just walk around and visit the sights. If you're traveling with someone it's a possibility they might not be as enthusiastic about blackjack as you are, and taking time out may be just what the doctor ordered. Don't have tunnel vision, open your eyes, and enjoy other opportunities that surround you.

THE POWER PLAY

This is for the other 10 percent (you know who you are). I developed this aspect of blackjack for the aggressive player. I do not recommend this for the beginner, only for someone who has been playing my system for some time and understands my five rules perfectly. Make no mistake; *the power play is not without risk.* However, the greater the risk, the greater the reward. My power play dictates that if you reach your win goal (50 percent of your bankroll), within the first hour, and you're not satisfied, this variation can yield 100 percent of your bankroll.

Let's begin. You have reached your 50 percent win goal, *within the first hour*; this indicates that you are on a hot trend, therefore by doubling your money

♠ ♦ ♣ ♥

management bet you can take advantage of this hot trend and go from a 50 percent to a 100 percent win in a very short period of time. What you are trying to do is ride the wave and hope it crests before it crashes.

You can use this formula with any table minimum. Let me show you an example: if you are playing at a $5 table and win $100 by using my money management system of 2-1-2-3-4-5-6 etc., your bets being $10-$5-$10-$15-$20-$25, to jump into the power play you simply begin doubling your bet to $20-$10-$20-$30-$40-$50, etc. By riding the wave of a hot trend you can realize a 100 percent win, in essence doubling your bankroll, in a short period of time. However, if the wave crashes, and you lose your 50 percent win, bringing you back to your original bankroll you must revert back to the original betting strategy of 2-1-2-3-4-5-6 or $10-$5-$10-$15-$20-$25. *Under no circumstances do you continue with the power play.* Your goal now is to get back to winning 50 percent of your bankroll.

At this time I wish to stress that the power play is only allowed once per session. It's acceptable to be aggressive, however I will not allow you to be stupid. Taking this risk more than once in a session is suicidal. I myself only use the power play under pristine conditions, which are rare! I'm not saying that I don't use the power play, but since I consider myself an investor not a gambler, I make certain to choose those times wisely.

♠ ♦ ♣ ♥

Beyond Recreation

"Can I make a living playing blackjack with your system?" Without a doubt this is my most frequently asked question, and originally I hadn't considered covering it, but I can't ignore the many cries for an answer. I would feel amiss writing this book without addressing this question. Let me be clear. The information and knowledge I share here was written for the occasional, recreational, and second-income-seeking blackjack players, or as I like to refer to them, investors. I did not foresee my system becoming someone's occupation. Playing blackjack for a living is not as pleasurable or as glamorous as you might expect. Before answering the question allow me to give you some of the downsides of becoming a professional blackjack player, and then you decide whether this lifestyle would make you comfortable.

First of all, to do this as a job you need a hefty bankroll, which I will talk about later. Second, it can become very stressful. Bear in mind you're not going to your primary job tomorrow, this is it—no steady paycheck, and security does not exist. Third, it is a very lonely existence shared by few, yet fantasized by many, and fourth it includes extensive travel.

If all this has not swayed your thinking, and you're determined to make this your way of life, rather than hold you back I will help you. I do feel, however, that it is my responsibility to warn you of the pitfalls. You'll probably never read another book or meet another author as blunt and honest as myself.

Having told you the truth, as I perceive it, I will now elaborate on the question first asked. The

♠ ◆ ♣ ♥

answer is yes, using my strategies and formula correctly will not only create you an occupation, it will also enhance your lifestyle above your wildest dreams. Yes, this can be true if a monetary goal is the summit of your heart. If this is true, here is the key to your success. If you have not already read my first book, *Blackjack's Hidden Secrets, Win Without Counting* you must do so now before attempting to go beyond recreational. That will be your foundation. Without the knowledge of my five basic rules you cannot hope to become successful as a professional. Every building needs a good foundation in order to withstand the test of time, you need to make certain yours will too.

Now, on to the money. In order to have an annual income of approximately $50,000 you need a bankroll of $25,000. Using my money management system, you must play at a $25 table with a $1000 bankroll per session, and also play five sessions a week, preferably one a day. With a 50 percent win goal and about an 80 percent win average, your income for the month should be $4000, or $1000 a week. If you desire an income of $100,000 a year yielding $2000 a week, your total bankroll should be $50,000. You need to play at a $50 table with a $2000 bankroll per session, playing five sessions per week. If your expectations per year are higher your bankroll needs to reflect that. How you declare this is your business. Incidentally, if you think I haven't done the math correctly, I've allowed time for a two-week vacation. Everybody needs a break.

Being a professional adds a different dimension to your game. Being good is unacceptable; being great is only good; only being perfect with my five rules is acceptable. Even being perfect, you will still lose about 20 percent of the time. Can you imagine what anything less than perfect would do to your new career where your only income is derived from playing blackjack? With this in mind I introduce another rule that while optional for the occasional, recreational, or second-income player, is an absolute must for the professional.

The rule goes like this: *Never alter your bankroll strategy mid-stream unless you have the backing to go with it.* If you are starting with a $25,000 total bankroll and hit a hot trend you are not permitted to increase your table minimum until you have PUT AWAY the required total bankroll for that table. Allow me to explain: with your $25,000 total bankroll you should be playing at a $25 table with $1000 per session, now you happen to win four or more times in a row and think "I should move to the $50 table 'cause I'm on a hot trend and I should take advantage of this." Don't do it. You have not accumulated enough bankroll to move to the next level of play. Upscaling to the $50 table requires you to have a total bankroll of $50,000 backing you. A few good trends are not enough to pull this off. Believe me, red-hot trends turn ice cold quickly. This run in trends is common and most players get cocky thinking they just can't lose.

The professional cannot afford the luxury of getting caught up in this illusion. I must stress that the level of play you start at is the level of play you must remain at, until your total bankroll reaches $50,000. When you reach that plateau you are permitted to make a decision to either stay at the $25,000 level, or raise your total bankroll to the $50,000 level, allowing you a larger annual income. You might say you've given yourself a raise for a job well done.

♠ ♦ ♣ ♥

I hope you have enjoyed reading this book as much as I have enjoyed writing it. It has been a pleasure sharing the knowledge it has taken me so long to acquire. See you at the tables.

♠ ♦ ♣ ♥

Blackjack Jargon

All professions have a jargon used in their occupation. Included here are terms found in this book (denoted in bold).

Bankroll or Bank   *the amount of gambling money the player brings to the casino.*

Card counting   *the ability of the player to keep track of how many 10 value cards are left in a shoe*

Color in   *to give your chips to a dealer in order for him or her to trade you up to higher valued chips. This is usually done right before leaving the table and cashing out at the cashier cage*

Comp   *short for complimentary, the privilege of using casino hotel services free of charge or at a discount.*

Double deck   *a blackjack game played with two decks of cards.*

Double down   *a move that allows a player to double his bet after looking at his first two cards. He is then dealt one additional card.*

Double exposure   *a blackjack game where both of the dealers cards are shown prior to the player playing his hand.*

Early surrender   *gives the player the opportunity to take back half his bet before the dealer checks to see whether he has blackjack.*

Final round   *the last round played in a blackjack tournament*

First base   *the first seat on the dealers left hand side.*

First player puck   *a device used during tournament play to keep track of which player bets first*

High roller   *a player whose average bet in blackjack for four hours in a 24 hour period is $100 or more.*

Insurance   *a side bet which is allowed when a dealer has an ace up card. The player may wager up to half of his original bet that the dealer's hole card is a ten.   If the dealer has blackjack, the house pays 2-to-1; if the dealer does not have blackjack, the player loses his side bet.*

♠ ♦ ♣ ♥

Intimidation   to make a player feel timid or afraid

Lamer   a clear plastic chip used to save a player's seat for approximately 20 minutes while he or she takes a break.

Late surrender   gives the player the opportunity to take back half his bet as long as the dealer does not have blackjack.

Multi blackjack   a house game that gives the casino a 20 percent vig.

Player card   a card, which resemble a credit card, that is issued by a casino in order to keep track of a players gambling time so that the player may be rated

Power play   a risky move that gives the player the ability to double his win goal

Rescue   similar to surrender but is only used in Spanish 21 to abandon your hand and receive back half your bet after doubling down.

Sessions   a period of time played at a table where you either meet your win goal or loss limit.

Single deck   a blackjack game played with one deck

Spanish 21   a house game, with no 10's in the deck, that gives the casino a 25 percent vig.

Split   an option allowing the player to make to cards of identical value into two hands, betting an amount equal to the original wager on the second card.

Spots   seats or playing space at a blackjack table

Table trends   the rhythms of the cards at a blackjack table.

Toke rate   the total amount of pooled dealer tips divided by the total amount of hours worked by all dealers.

Unit   a betting increment

VIP   Very important player

♠ ♦ ♣ ♥

Order Form

Quantity	Description	Unit Price	Total
_____	Blackjack's Hidden Secrets II	$12.95	_____
_____	Surrender Rules Card	$2.00	_____

Other publications by George Pappadopoulos

Quantity	Description	Unit Price	Total
_____	Blackjack's Hidden Secrets	$11.95	_____
_____	Laminated Cheat Sheet	$2.00	_____

Shipping and Handling Charges

$4 per book (U.S. only), $1 per card (U.S. only).
Contact us for other rates. UPS 2nd Day Air available for an additional $10 per shipping address.

Please allow 2 to 4 weeks for delivery.

Total amount for items _____

(NJ residents add 6% Sales Tax) _____

*Shipping and Handling _____

Total enclosed _____

Name _____

Address _____

City_____State_____ Zip_____

Daytime tel. # (_____) _____ (*in case we have a question about your order*)

Method of payment:

❏ Check or Money Order (U.S. Funds)   ❏ Visa   ❏ MC   ❏ Discover   ❏ American Express

Credit Card #_____ Exp. date_____

Name on Card_____

Authorized Signature_____

Credit card orders may include email address for order confirmation.

Mail form to:

ME-n-U Marketers

P.O. Box 127, Linwood, NJ 08221

phone 609-653-3069 or fax 609-653-8186

55